little grasshopper books™

Bible Stories

Get the App!

1. Download the Little Grasshopper Library App* from the App Store or Google Play. Find direct links to store locations at **www.littlegrasshopperbooks.com**

2. Open the app and tap the **+ Add Book** button at the bottom of the screen.**

3. Line up the QR Code Scanner with one of the QR codes found in this book. Each story will automatically start downloading to your app!

4. Be sure to accept any prompts that come up.

5. Information on device compatibility and troubleshooting can be found at **www.littlegrasshopperbooks.com**

Illustrated by: Stacy Peterson
Bible stories adapted by: Beth Taylor
Additional text: traditional hymns, psalms and folk songs
Scripture quotations from *The Holy Bible, King James Version*
App content developed in partnership with Filament Games.

Louis Weber, CEO
Publications International, Ltd.
8140 Lehigh Avenue
Morton Grove, IL 60053

ISBN: 978-1-64030-985-2
Manufactured in China.
8 7 6 5 4 3 2 1

*We reserve the right to terminate the apps.
**Smartphone not included. Standard data rates may apply to download. Once the app and an individual book's content are downloaded, the app does not use data or require Wi-Fi access.

Table of Contents

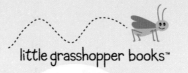

little grasshopper books™

David and Goliath

Once there was a shepherd boy named David. He watched over his father's sheep. David was the youngest and smallest of his brothers.

A king named Saul was ruler of the Israelites. David and his family were Israelites too. The Israelites were fighting with another group of people called the Philistines.

David's older brothers were going off to fight. But David was too young. After helping them pack, he stayed home.

One day David's father asked him to take food to his older brothers, who were soldiers in King Saul's army.

"Visit the Israelite camp," said David's father. "And come back with news about how your brothers are doing."

"I will," David said.

King Saul's army was camped on one side of a valley. The Philistine army was gathered on the other side of the valley.

David searched among Saul's soldiers until he found two of his brothers.

"What are you doing here?" asked David's oldest brother. "This is no place for boys," his other brother said. "You should be at home with the sheep."

Just then, a giant soldier from the Philistine army stepped forward. He was nearly ten feet tall.

"I am Goliath," the giant roared. "Who is brave enough to fight me?"

None of King Saul's soldiers answered.
They were all too afraid.
David was not afraid of Goliath.
"I will fight the giant," David said.

David went to King Saul and told him that he would fight Goliath.

"But you are just a boy," King Saul said. "And Goliath is a great warrior."

David told the king about how he protected his father's sheep. Finally, King Saul agreed to let David fight the giant.

King Saul gave David a sword and armor to protect him. But the armor was too big.

"I cannot move in this," David said. "I will fight without armor."

David went to the stream and gathered several stones for his sling.

When Goliath saw David approaching with only a sling, the giant laughed.

"You cannot beat me," Goliath said. "You are just a boy."

"You are bigger than me," David said. "But God is on my side."

David placed a stone in his sling and sent it flying through the air. It hit Goliath right between the eyes. Goliath fell down to the ground with a loud thud.

When the Philistines saw Goliath
fall, they turned and ran away.

The Israelites cheered David for saving his people.
Years later, David became king of Israel.

Hear Us, Holy Jesus

Jesus, from your throne on high,
Far above the bright blue sky,
Look on us with loving eye.
Hear us, holy Jesus.

Please be with us every day,
In our work and in our play,
When we learn and when we pray.
Hear us, holy Jesus.

Morning Prayer

For this new morning with its light,
For rest and shelter of the night,
For health and food, for love and friends,
For everything your goodness sends,
We thank you, dearest Lord. Amen.

Michael, Row the Boat Ashore

Michael, row the boat ashore, Hallelujah!
Michael, row the boat ashore, Hallelujah!

The river is deep and the river is wide, Hallelujah!
Milk and honey on the other side, Hallelujah!

Jordan's river is chilly and cold, Hallelujah!
Chills the body but warms the soul, Hallelujah!

Jesus, Help Me

Jesus, help my eyes to see
All the good that you send me.
Jesus, help my ears to hear
Calls for help from far and near.

Jesus, help my feet to go
In the way that you will show.
Jesus, help my hands to do
All things loving, kind, and true.
Jesus, may I helpful be,
Growing every day like thee. Amen.

All Things Bright and Beautiful

All things bright and beautiful,
All creatures great and small,
All things wise and wonderful:
The Lord God made them all.
He gave us eyes to see them,
And lips that we might tell
How great is God Almighty,
Who has made all things well.

Be Near Me, Lord Jesus

Be near me, Lord Jesus,
I ask you to stay
Close by me forever,
And love me, I pray.

Bless all the dear children
In your tender care,
And take us to heaven
To live with you there.

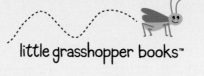

Noah and the Ark

Once there was a man named Noah. Noah loved God. Noah also loved his family and neighbors. This made God happy.

But God was unhappy with the people in the rest of the world.

God said to Noah, "I am going to wash away everything bad with a great flood."

God told Noah to build a big boat called an ark to save his family.

"Bring two of every kind of animal onto the ark," God said. "And bring plenty of food for everyone."

Noah and his family started building the ark right away. Noah's neighbors laughed when they saw what his family was building.

"Why do you need a big boat?" one neighbor chuckled. "You live in the desert!"

Noah warned other people about the flood, but no one listened.

Noah and his family worked on the ark day and night. Finally, the ark was finished.

Then Noah's family gathered food to bring on the ark. They picked fruits, vegetables, and nuts. They stored enough food on the ark to feed Noah's family and the animals for a long time.

Noah gathered two of every kind of animal as God told him.

The animals lined up in pairs. They boarded the ark two by two.

Once Noah and his family were safely on board the ark with the animals, it started to rain.

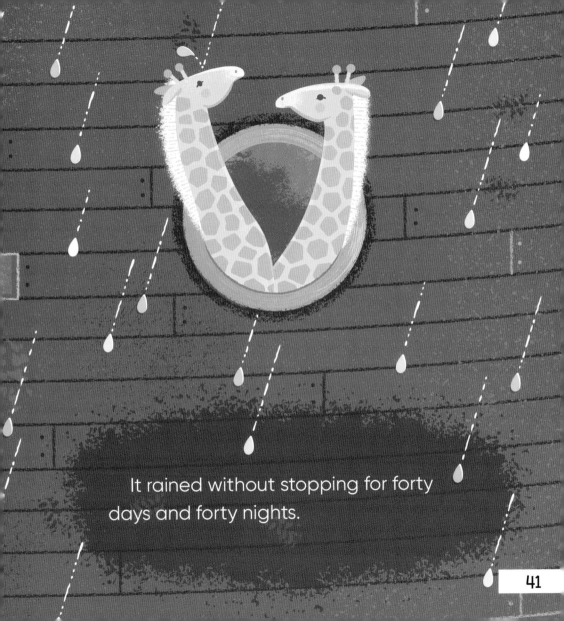

It rained without stopping for forty days and forty nights.

Soon water covered the entire Earth. Even the tallest mountains were underwater. Inside the ark the people and animals were safe.

After the rain stopped, the water slowly started to go down. The ark came to rest on top of a mountain.

Noah sent out a dove to search for dry land.

The dove returned with a new olive leaf. This showed Noah that the land was dry and plants were growing again.

Noah knew it was finally safe to leave the ark. He and his family unloaded the animals onto dry land.

All the animals found new homes. The land was full of beautiful plants.

God promised Noah he would never again flood the entire Earth.

"Whenever you see a rainbow in the sky," God said, "remember my promise."

A Prayer for Guidance

All through the day,

I humbly pray,

Please be my guard and guide.

My sins forgive,

And let me live,

Blessed Jesus, by your side. Amen.

Count Your Blessings

Count your blessings, name them one by one.

Count your blessings, see what God has done.

Count your blessings, name them one by one.

Count your many blessings, see what God has done.

When upon life's billows you are tempest-tossed,
When you are discouraged, thinking all is lost,
Count your many blessings, name them one by one,
And it will surprise you what the Lord has done.

Angel of God

Angel of God,
my guardian dear,
To whom God's love
Permits me here,
Ever this day
Be at my side,
To light and guard,
To rule and guide. Amen.

Keep Me, Jesus

Keep my little tongue today,
Keep it gentle while I play.
Keep my hands from doing wrong,
Keep my feet the whole day long.
Keep me all, oh Jesus mild,
Keep me ever your dear child. Amen.

This Little Light of Mine

This little light of mine,
I'm gonna let it shine.
This little light of mine,
I'm gonna let it shine.
This little light of mine,
I'm gonna let it shine,
Let it shine, shine, shine,
Oh let it shine.

Everywhere I go,

I'm gonna let it shine.

Everywhere I go,

I'm gonna let it shine.

Everywhere I go,

I'm gonna let it shine,

Let it shine, shine, shine,

Oh let it shine.

Jonah and the Whale

Once there was a man named Jonah. When God spoke, Jonah listened. Then Jonah spread God's message to other people.

One day God told Jonah to go to the city of Nineveh. "Tell the people of Nineveh to stop being bad," said God. "They need to obey my rules."

But Jonah did not want to go to Nineveh. Instead he ran away.

Jonah boarded a ship going far away from Nineveh.
He fell fast asleep below the ship's deck.

While he was asleep, God sent a mighty storm to get Jonah's attention. God was angry at Jonah for disobeying him. The waves crashed and the wind blew, but still Jonah slept.

The storm got worse and worse. The sailors were afraid the ship would break apart. They all cried out to their gods to save them. But the storm raged on.

"Throw the cargo overboard," the captain yelled.
So the sailors threw the cargo into the sea. But the storm only grew stronger.

Finally, the captain went below deck to wake Jonah. "How can you sleep in a storm like this?" asked the captain. "Pray to your God to save us!"

Then Jonah realized the storm was a message from God.

Jonah knew it was his fault the ship was caught in such
a terrible storm.

"Throw me overboard," said Jonah. "Then the storm will
calm down."

The sailors threw Jonah into the sea. The storm suddenly calmed down.

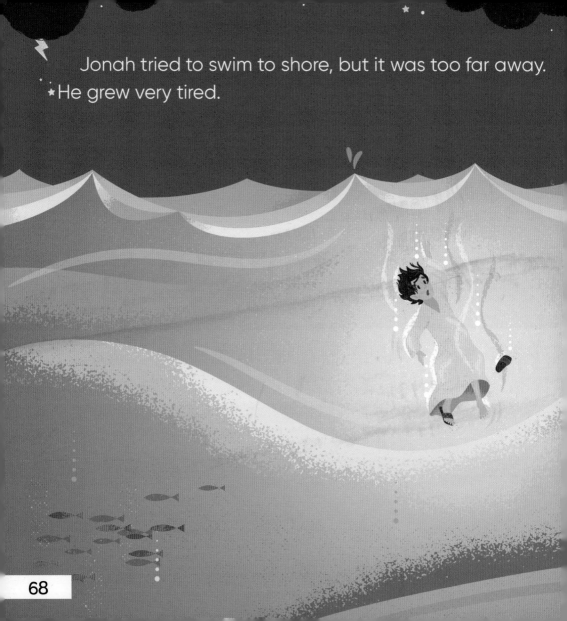

Jonah tried to swim to shore, but it was too far away. He grew very tired.

Just as Jonah sank beneath the waves, God sent a giant whale to save him. The whale swallowed Jonah whole.

Inside the belly of the whale, it was cold and smelly. Jonah was afraid.

So he prayed to God. Jonah asked God for forgiveness for not going to Nineveh. He prayed for God's help to get out of the whale.

After three days, God answered Jonah's prayer.
The whale spat Jonah out onto dry land.

Jonah thanked God for saving his life.

Jonah finally went to Nineveh. He told the people all about God. They listened and changed their ways.

The Lord's Prayer

Our Father which art in heaven,

Hallowed be thy name.

Thy kingdom come, thy will be done in earth,

As it is in heaven.

Give us this day our daily bread,

And forgive us our debts, as we forgive our debtors.

And lead us not into temptation, but deliver us from evil:

For thine is the kingdom,

And the power, and the glory, for ever.

Amen.

A Prayer Before Meals

We thank you, heavenly Father,
For every earthly good,
For life, and health, and clothing,
And for our daily food.

Give us hearts to thank you
For every blessing sent,
And for whatever you send us,
May we always be content. Amen.

A Prayer for Courage

As a little child relies
On a care beyond his own,
Knows he's neither strong nor wise,
Fears to stir a step alone—
Let me thus with you abide,
As my father, guard, and guide. Amen.

Jesus Loves Me

Jesus loves me, this I know,
For the Bible tells me so!
Little ones to him belong,
They are weak, but he is strong.

Yes, Jesus loves me!
Yes, Jesus loves me!
Yes, Jesus loves me!
The Bible tells me so.

We Are Little Children

We are little children,
Very young indeed.
But the savior's promise
Each of us may plead.

If we seek him early,
If we come today,
We can be his little friends.
He has said we may.

All Through the Night

Sleep, my child, and peace attend you,
All through the night.
Guardian angels God will send you,
All through the night.
Soft the drowsy hours are creeping,
Hill and vale in slumber sleeping,
I my loving vigil keeping,
All through the night.

While the moon her watch is keeping,
All through the night;
While the weary world is sleeping,
All through the night;
Over your spirit gently stealing,
Visions of delight revealing,
Breathes a pure and holy feeling,
All through the night.

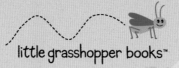

Daniel and the Lions

Once there was a man named Daniel who loved God.
Daniel prayed to God every day.

King Darius liked Daniel. He chose Daniel as one of his three advisers to help him rule the kingdom. Daniel worked hard and soon became the king's favorite.

"I think I will put Daniel in charge of everything,"
King Darius said one day.

The other advisers were jealous of Daniel.

"Who does Daniel think he is?" one moaned. "Why should he be in charge of everything?"

"I wish he would make a big mistake," grumbled the other. "Then we could get rid of him!"
So the advisers made an evil plan.

The two advisers went to see King Darius.

"You are such a great and wise king," one cried. "You are like a god."

"You should make a new law," the other suggested. "Everyone must pray only to you. If anyone breaks the law, they will be thrown in the lions' den."

King Darius agreed to make the law.

When Daniel heard about the law, he thought the other advisers might be trying to get rid of him. But Daniel still prayed to God as he always did.

The two mean advisers were delighted when they caught Daniel praying to God instead of to King Darius. They rushed off to tell the king.

"Daniel has broken the law!" one exclaimed.
"Throw him in the lions' den!" the other cried.

King Darius was sorry for making the law. He realized it was a trick to get rid of Daniel. He did not want to throw Daniel in the lions' den. But the law had to be obeyed.

"I am sorry, but you must be punished," King Darius told Daniel with tears in his eyes. "I hope your God will protect you."

Daniel was thrown into the lions' den. He kept his faith in God. Daniel prayed to God to keep him safe.

All night long, King Darius worried about Daniel. He could not eat or sleep. Early the next morning, the king rushed to the lions' den.

"Daniel, has your God saved you from the lions?" the king shouted nervously.

"Yes," Daniel replied. "God kept me safe, because he knew I did nothing wrong."

Daniel climbed out of the lions' den. He did not have a single scratch! The king was amazed that God saved Daniel.

King Darius knew the mean advisers had tricked him into punishing Daniel. So the king punished the bad men.

King Darius made a new law for everyone in the kingdom to respect God. Daniel returned to helping the king rule again.

Go Tell It on the Mountain

Go tell it on the mountain,
Over the hills and everywhere;
Go tell it on the mountain
That Jesus Christ is born.

Down in a lowly manger,
The humble Christ was born,
And God sent us salvation
That blessed Christmas morn.

A Prayer for Help

Tender Jesus,
Meek and mild,
Look on me,
A little child.
Help me,
If it is your will,
To recover
From all ill. Amen.

Come, Holy Spirit

Come, Holy Spirit, come,
Let your bright beams arise.
Dispel the darkness from our minds,
And open all our eyes.

Revive our drooping faith,
Our doubts and fears remove,
And kindle in us the flame
Of everlasting love. Amen.

Joyful, Joyful, We Adore You

Joyful, joyful, we adore you,
God of glory, lord of love.
Hearts unfold like flowers before you,
Opening to the sun above.
Melt the clouds of sin and sadness,
Drive the dark of doubt away.
Giver of immortal gladness,
Fill us with the light of day!

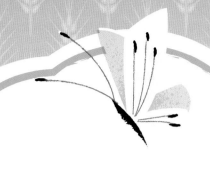

All your works with joy surround you,
Earth and heaven reflect your rays.
Stars and angels sing around you,
Center of unbroken praise.
Field and forest, valley and mountain,
Flowery meadow, flashing sea,
Chanting bird and flowing fountain
Praising you eternally!

Down to the River to Pray

As I went down to the river to pray,
Studying about that good old way
And who shall wear the starry crown,
Good Lord, show me the way.

O children, let's go down,
Let's go down, come on down.
O children, let's go down,
Down to the river to pray.

He's Got the Whole World

He's got the whole world in his hands.
He's got the whole world in his hands.
He's got the whole world in his hands.
He's got the whole world in his hands.

He's got the wind and the rain in his hands.
He's got the wind and the rain in his hands.
He's got the wind and the rain in his hands.
He's got the whole world in his hands.

Joseph and His Colorful Coat

There once was a boy named Joseph. He had many brothers. Joseph and his brothers watched over their father's sheep.

Their father, Jacob, loved Joseph best. One day Jacob gave Joseph a present. It was a beautiful coat made of many colors.

"My favorite son deserves a special coat," Jacob said.

"I love it," said Joseph.

Joseph wore his special coat everywhere. This made Joseph's brothers angry because they wanted special coats too.

Whenever Joseph saw his brothers do something wrong, he would tell their father.

His brothers were mad at Joseph for getting them in trouble. Everything Joseph did made his brothers upset.

One day while they watched the sheep, Joseph told his brothers about a dream he had.

"Each of us had a bunch of grain," Joseph said. "Then my bunch stood up. All of your bunches of grain bowed down to me."

This made his brothers even more angry than Joseph's special coat.

"Do you think you are better than us?" one brother asked.

"Last night I had another dream," Joseph told his brothers a few days later.

"The sun, moon, and stars bowed down to me," Joseph said. "Someday you will all bow down to me."

Joseph's brothers were furious.
"We will never bow down to you," said one brother.

Jacob sent Joseph to check on his brothers, who were far away tending sheep.

Joseph's brothers saw him in his colorful coat from a distance.

"Here comes the dreamer boy," one brother said. "We should get rid of him."

When Joseph arrived, his brothers ripped off his special coat. They threw him in an empty well.

"We shall see what comes of your dreams now," his brothers shouted into the well.

The brothers sat down to eat their dinner. As they were eating, they saw some travelers coming along.

"Let us sell our little brother to these traveling merchants,"
suggested one brother.

So the brothers sold Joseph to the merchants who were
traveling to Egypt.

The brothers returned home with Joseph's colorful coat.
"Where is Joseph?" their father asked.

"We do not know," said one brother.

"We found his coat ripped up," said another brother.

"He must have been eaten by a wild animal."

Jacob was very sad. He missed Joseph.

After many years in Egypt, Joseph met his family again. He forgave his brothers and was again part of his family.

Take My Heart

Come, dearest savior, take my heart,

And let me never from you depart.

Amen.

Faithful Shepherd

Faithful shepherd, feed me
In the pastures green.
Faithful shepherd, lead me
Where your steps are seen.

Daily bring me nearer
To the heavenly shore.
May my faith grow clearer.
May I love you more!

A Prayer Before Learning

Blessed Lord, let your blessing go with me today. Help me be obedient to my teachers and learn with pleasure whatever I am taught, to your great honor and glory. Amen.

Oh Happy Day

Oh happy day that fixed my choice
On you, my savior and my God.
Well may this glowing heart rejoice,
And tell its raptures all abroad.

Happy day, happy day,
When Jesus washed my sins away!
He taught me how to watch and pray,
And live rejoicing every day.
Happy day, happy day,
When Jesus washed my sins away.

Moses and Miriam

Long ago, the Egyptians and Israelites lived happily together in Egypt. Then a bad Pharaoh came to power. He made the Israelites slaves.

The Pharaoh was unhappy. He thought there were too many Israelite slaves. So the Pharaoh gave a terrible order.

"Take every Israelite boy that is born away from his mother," the Pharaoh told his guards. "From now on, the Israelites may only have daughters."

Around this time there was an Israelite woman called Jochebed. She had a daughter named Miriam.

Jochebed gave birth to a baby boy, Moses. To keep Moses safe, Jochebed and Miriam made a plan.

Jochebed sent Miriam to the river to collect reeds.

Together, Jochebed and Miriam wove a sturdy basket from the reeds. They covered it with tar to make it waterproof.

Jochebed put Moses in the basket and gave it to Miriam.

"Go to the river and hide the basket among the reeds," Jochebed told Miriam.

"Stay nearby," she told Miriam, "and watch over your brother."

"I will," Miriam promised.

Miriam watched as the basket floated toward some women who were swimming in the river. One of them was a princess, the Pharaoh's daughter.

The princess saw the basket and looked inside.
Just then Moses started to cry.

The princess was kind and felt sorry for him.
"He is one of the Israelite babies," the
princess said.

Miriam rushed over to the princess.

"Should I find a nurse to look after the baby for you?" Miriam asked.

"Yes," the princess answered.

Miriam ran to fetch her mother and brought her to the princess.

"Will you take care of this baby for me?" the princess asked Jochebed.

"Yes!" Jochebed happily agreed. She would be able to care for her own son.

Jochebed and Miriam thanked God that Moses was safe. They took Moses home.

When Moses was old enough, Jochebed brought him to the princess at the Pharaoh's palace. The princess adopted Moses and raised him as her own son.

Moses grew up as a prince of Egypt, but he never forgot his own people. Years later, he led the Israelites to freedom.

At the Close of Every Day

At the close of every day,
Lord, to you I kneel and pray.
Look upon your little child,
Look in love and mercy mild.
Please forgive and wash away
All my naughtiness this day.
And both when I sleep and wake,
Bless me for my savior's sake.

Shall We Gather at the River

Shall we gather at the river,
Where bright angel feet have trod,
With its crystal tide forever
Flowing by the throne of God?

Yes, we'll gather at the river,
The beautiful, the beautiful river.
Gather with the saints at the river
That flows by the throne of God.

On the margin of the river,
Washing up its silver spray,
We will walk and worship ever,
All the happy golden day.

Yes, we'll gather at the river,
The beautiful, the beautiful river.
Gather with the saints at the river
That flows by the throne of God.

You Are Wherever We Go

Lord, you are here,
Lord, you are there.
You are wherever we go.
Lord, you guide us,
Lord, you protect us.
You are wherever we go.
Lord, we need you,
Lord, we trust you,
You are wherever we go.
Lord, we love you,
Lord, we praise you,
You are wherever we go.

A Prayer of Thanks

For the new morning
With its light,
For rest and shelter
Of the night,
For health and food,
For love and friends,
For everything
Your goodness sends,
We thank you, dearest Lord. Amen.

Amazing Grace

Amazing grace, how sweet the sound,
That saved a wretch like me.
I once was lost, but now I'm found,
Was blind, but now I see.

It was grace that taught my heart to fear,
And grace my fears relieved.
How precious did that grace appear
The hour I first believed!

God Made

God made the sun,
God made the trees,
God made the mountains,
And God made me!
Thank you, oh God,
For the sun and the trees,
For making the mountains,
And for making me!

Go Down, Moses

When Israel was in Egypt's land,
Let my people go,
Oppressed so hard they could not stand,
Let my people go.

Go down, Moses,
Way down in Egypt's land.
Tell old Pharaoh:
Let my people go.

Lord, help us all from bondage flee,
Let my people go,
And let us all in Christ be free,
Let my people go,

Go down, Moses,
Way down in Egypt's land.
Tell old Pharaoh:
Let my people go.

Bedtime Prayer

The day is done.
Oh God the son,
Look down upon
Your little one!

I need not fear
If you are near.
You are my Savior
Kind and dear. Amen.